Mountain PR: A Journey to Marketing Greatness

An Expedition Guide to Branding, Client Attraction, and Business Success

Mountain PR: A Journey to Marketing Greatness

An Expedition Guide to Branding, Client Attraction, and Business Success

Maria Koussertari Martin

Copyright © 2024 by **Maria Koussertari Martin**

All rights reserved. No part of this book may be used or reproduced by any means, graphic, electronic, or mechanical, including photocopying, recording, taping, or by any information storage retrieval system, without the written permission of the publisher except in the case of brief quotations embodied in critical articles and reviews.

Contents

Introduction 1

Chapter 1: Plan Your Journey 3

Chapter 2: Flag Your Route 7

Chapter 3: Marketing and Content 9

Chapter 4: Client Attraction and Retention 11

Chapter 5: Consistency is Key 13

Conclusion: The Journey to Greatness Continues 15

About the Author 17

Acknowledgments 19

Contact Information 20

Introduction

Welcome to *Mountain PR: A Journey to Marketing Greatness*. Whether you're a business owner, freelancer, or someone looking to establish a personal brand, this book is your trusted guide to navigating the mountains of marketing, client attraction, and business success. Just like climbing a mountain, building a successful brand requires careful planning, resilience, and the right tools.

The journey of business can be daunting, and many entrepreneurs get lost along the way. This book will give you the strategies to map your route and overcome the obstacles that may arise on your path to greatness.

Each chapter in this book mirrors the stages of an expedition. You'll learn how to prepare yourself mentally and strategically, attract the right clients, and build long-lasting relationships that fuel your success. By the end, you'll be well-equipped to scale your business to new heights.

CHAPTER 1

Plan Your Journey

Base Camp: Discovering Your True North

Before you can reach the summit of success, you must prepare yourself for the journey ahead. This starts with self-awareness—your compass for navigating the business world. The most successful entrepreneurs are those who have a deep understanding of their own strengths and weaknesses, values, and beliefs.

Understanding Yourself: Mapping Your Traits

Imagine you're at base camp, preparing for the climb ahead. Every climber knows they need to assess their gear and physical condition before ascending. In business, your personal traits are your most important tools. Reflect on your strengths and what roles you naturally excel in. Consider the following roles that every entrepreneur plays:

- **The Creative**: Do you thrive on ideas and innovation? Creatives are often great at designing new products, developing unique marketing campaigns, or finding unconventional solutions.

- **The Visionary**: Do you have a clear long-term goal? Visionaries can see the future of their business and inspire others to follow their direction.

- **The Negotiator**: Are you good at making deals and building partnerships? Negotiators excel at forming mutually beneficial relationships.

- **The Customer Service Manager**: Do you prioritise client satisfaction and communication? If so, this role might come naturally to you.

- **The Marketing and Sales Guru**: Are you skilled at promoting your products or services? Marketing-minded entrepreneurs know how to draw attention to their business and convert leads into clients.

PRACTICAL EXERCISE: SELF-AWARENESS CHECKLIST

Use the following checklist to identify which traits resonate most with you. Write down your top three and reflect on how you can leverage them in your business.

- Are you a creative thinker or a strategist?
- Do you prefer working solo or leading a team?
- What are your core values, and how do they influence your business decisions?

Choosing Your Path: The Problem You Will Solve

Now that you have a clear understanding of your traits and strengths, it's time to define your business's purpose. The most successful businesses solve specific problems for their clients. Ask yourself:

- **What problem do I want to solve?**
- **Who is my target audience?**
- **How will my unique skills and strengths help me solve this problem?**

Consider writing down a mission statement that reflects your core purpose. This mission will serve as your guide throughout the journey ahead, helping you stay aligned with your values and goals.

CHAPTER 2

FLAG YOUR ROUTE

CAMP 1: CRAFTING YOUR OFFER

You've identified your purpose and path—now it's time to create an offer that will guide your clients along the journey with you. This step is all about crafting an irresistible offer that solves your clients' problems in a way they cannot refuse.

CREATING AN IRRESISTIBLE OFFER

An effective offer is clear, concise, and focuses on value. Here's a framework for building an offer that resonates with your audience:

- **Identify the Core Problem**: Understand the pain points of your target audience. What specific problem do they face that your product or service can solve?

- **Emphasise the Solution**: Clearly explain how your product or service will solve that problem. Use simple, direct language to communicate the benefits.

- **Highlight the Transformation**: Paint a picture of the results your clients will experience after they use your solution. Will they save time? Make more money? Experience peace of mind?

Example of a Clear Offer

For instance, if you're a marketing consultant, your offer might look like this:

"I help small businesses increase their online visibility through SEO strategies and content marketing. In just 60 days, you'll see a 30% increase in website traffic and improved customer engagement."

The Power of Messaging

No matter how great your offer is, if you don't communicate it clearly, it will fall flat. Use storytelling techniques to connect emotionally with your audience. Incorporate these messaging tips into your offer:

- **Use Visuals**: Consider creating an infographic that outlines the benefits of your offer. Visuals often speak louder than words.
- **Add a Personal Touch**: Use testimonials and success stories from previous clients to build credibility.

Practical Exercise: Craft Your Offer

Using the framework above, draft an offer that clearly communicates the problem you solve and the value you provide. Share it with a colleague or mentor to get feedback and refine it.

CHAPTER 3

Marketing and Content

Camp 2: Engaging and Effective Content

Content creation is the lifeblood of any marketing strategy. Without engaging and consistent content, your audience may lose interest or never even discover your business. In this chapter, we will explore how to create content that not only engages but converts.

Timing and Consistency: The Key to Visibility

Imagine planting flags along your route. Each piece of content you release is a flag that keeps clients on track, moving toward your offer. To keep your business top-of-mind, it's crucial to release content at regular intervals.

- **Set a Content Schedule**: Create a content calendar where you plan out your posts, emails, or videos for the next month. Consistency builds trust, so aim to post regularly.

- **Experiment with Different Mediums**: Try a variety of formats, such as blog posts, social media updates, podcasts, or YouTube videos, to see which resonates most with your audience.

Being Authentic in Content Creation

Clients crave authenticity. They want to feel like they're connecting with a real person, not a faceless company. Don't worry about perfect grammar or corporate-sounding language. Instead, focus on being genuine and relatable.

- **Tell Your Story**: Share the struggles and successes of your own journey in business. Clients will relate to your experiences and feel more connected to your brand.
- **Share Behind-the-Scenes Content**: Show clients what goes on behind the scenes in your business. This could be a day-in-the-life video, a post about your team, or a sneak peek at a new product you're launching.

Practical Exercise: Plan Your Content Strategy

Create a simple content calendar for the next month. Plan out one piece of content per week and set a goal for how it will engage or educate your audience.

Chapter 4

Client Attraction and Retention

The Summit: Reaching the Top

Congratulations! You've now reached the summit of your marketing mountain. Clients are discovering your business, and they're following the path you've laid out for them. But the journey doesn't end here. At the summit, your focus shifts to building trust and fostering long-term relationships with your clients.

Building Long-Term Relationships

Your clients are your most valuable asset, and retaining them should be your priority. Here are strategies to deepen relationships with clients:

- **Personalised Communication**: Use their names in emails and recognise their milestones. A simple "Congratulations on your 1-year anniversary with us!" can go a long way.

- **Exclusive Offers**: Offer special discounts or early access to new products for loyal clients.

- **Regular Check-ins**: Schedule periodic calls or emails just to see how your clients are doing with your product or service.

Example: Retaining Clients through Personalisation

One company noticed that its repeat clients had higher lifetime value than new customers, so they started sending personalised holiday gifts to top clients. The gesture not only strengthened client loyalty but also increased referrals.

Practical Exercise: Implement a Client Retention Strategy

Identify your top three clients and plan a personalised communication or gift for them in the next month. Track their responses to see if it improves engagement or leads to referrals.

CHAPTER 5

Consistency is Key

Navigating the Descent: Maintaining Profitability

The climb down the mountain requires as much care and focus as the ascent. Maintaining profitability in your business depends on consistency. Just as climbers need to maintain their balance on the descent, entrepreneurs need to keep their processes streamlined and efficient.

Using Technology to Streamline Your Business

Automation tools can be a game changer in maintaining consistency:

- **Social Media Automation**: Use tools like Buffer or Hootsuite to schedule posts in advance.
- **Email Marketing**: Set up automated email funnels that nurture leads without constant oversight.
- **CRM Tools**: Implement a customer relationship management (CRM) system to track interactions and sales pipelines.

Practical Exercise: Identify Areas for Automation

List the repetitive tasks in your business and research one tool that could automate each task. Implement at least one automation in the next week.

CONCLUSION

THE JOURNEY TO GREATNESS CONTINUES

You've reached the top of the mountain, but as any great explorer knows, the journey to greatness never truly ends. There are always new peaks to conquer and new lessons to learn. Keep pushing forward, keep refining your skills, and keep building your brand.

Success is not a single destination—it's the culmination of your continued effort, persistence, and passion. With every step, you're moving closer to your next summit.

Now it's your turn. Take the first step today and start your journey to marketing greatness. Don't just dream about the view from the top—experience it for yourself!

ABOUT THE AUTHOR

I am a passionate advocate for equality, diversity, and empowerment for women, fueled by a deep appreciation for the beauty of culture and the great outdoors. As a creative digital marketer and journalist, I proudly represent the millennial generation, harnessing the power of the digital landscape to amplify my voice and connect with a vibrant community.

My passion project, *Athena Women Today*, is a dynamic video podcast that shines a spotlight on the journeys of remarkable women who are breaking barriers and redefining confidence in today's world. Each episode features in-depth, engaging interviews, allowing trailblazing women to share their inspiring stories of building self-confidence, overcoming challenges, and navigating personal and professional landscapes with grace and resilience.

As the heart behind *Write Side of Her*, I explore themes of acceptance, diversity, and empowerment. Through my personal blog series, I share my own experiences in education, careers, and motherhood, offering fresh perspectives that inspire meaningful conversations and encourage us all to embrace our unique journeys.

Author of *Wild Kid Books*, I ignite a passion for nature in young children through vibrant, rhyming illustrated stories, inspiring the next generation to cherish and protect our planet.

Through my company, *Mountain PR (.co.uk)*, I empower individuals and businesses by delivering exceptional marketing, content creation, and coaching services that propel them toward success.

As a PADI Advanced Scuba Diver, I am on a mission to explore the depths of the ocean while advocating for critical ocean conservation efforts.

When I'm not diving or crafting compelling stories, you can find me dancing in stiletto heels, quite literally staying on my toes and embracing life to the fullest!

Acknowledgments

Thank you to everyone who supported me on this journey, including my amazing husband Shane and the "Out of Towners" ladies: Holly Mercer, Leanne Gray and Lauren Read, who really did climb a mountain with me.

Contact Information

Reach out to begin a conversation on how I can help you climb your business or personal mountains. Connect with me at: **mountainpr.co.uk**

What Clients Say

Claire McAllister

"Maria is a tour de force. You need Maria in your life if you are looking for holistic marketing and web design, support and guidance. As a musician, writer and life coach I told her I needed someone to hold my hand, through the scary world of online presence and marketing. She did that and more. Her nurturing, empathic and empowering presence has helped me now feel empowered and enabled in my own business, as well as learning so much about marketing. The cherry on the cake is that our business relationship has blossomed into friendship too."

www.ingramcontent.com/pod-product-compliance
Lightning Source LLC
Chambersburg PA
CBHW040306220526
45473CB00002B/594